THE GREAT BOOK OF ANIMAL KNOWLEDGE

# CHIMPANZEES

The Smartest Primates on the Planet

# Introduction

The chimpanzee is a type of ape that lives in Africa. They are the closest animals related to humans in the world. Chimpanzees live in large groups and they are one of the animals that like to groom each other. Chimpanzees are a well known animal, but sadly, they are endangered. This means that they are slowly starting to disappear from the wild. Chimpanzees are intelligent animals. In fact, they know how to use tools! Let's learn more about the chimpanzee!

# What the Chimpanzee Looks Like

Photo by William Warby (flickr.com/wwarby), as licensed under CC BY 2.0 Generic

Of all the animals in the world, chimpanzees look the closest to humans. They have long arms and legs. They are covered with long black hair except their ears, fingers, toes and face. Chimpanzees have five fingers that they use for picking up and holding things. Chimpanzees also use their toes to grasp things. One of the main differences between a chimpanzee and other monkeys is chimpanzees do not have tails.

# Size

Photo by Kevin Wheeler (flickr.com/kevwheeler), as licensed under CC BY 2.0 Generic

Chimpanzees are smaller than average humans. Females can grow 2 to 3.5 feet tall and they weigh around 60 to 110 pounds. Male chimpanzees are larger than females. They grow 3 to 4 feet tall and can weigh 90 to 115 pounds.

# Movement

Chimpanzees usually walk on all four limbs like most land mammals. But they can also walk upright like humans! They walk on two feet if they need their hands to carry something, but they don't usually walk this way. Chimpanzees are also very good at climbing trees. They use their hands to swing from branch to branch.

# Where the Chimpanzee Lives

Photo by Afrika Force (flickr.com/afrikaforce), as licensed under CC BY 2.0 Generic

Wild chimpanzees can be found only in Africa. They are located in central and western Africa. Chimpanzees can mostly be found in rainforests and wet savannas. They spend an equal amount of time in land and on trees. But they do most of their feeding and sleeping on trees.

# Nests

Chimpanzees don't hang from trees while they sleep. Instead, they build nests. Chimpanzees build bowl shaped nests made out of some branches, twigs, and leaves to soften it a little. Chimpanzees curl in their nest when it's time to sleep. Each chimpanzee has their own nest except mothers who share their nest with their young. Mothers also teach their young chimpanzees how to build their own nests.

# Groups

Photo by Klaus Post (flickr.com/klauspost), as licensed under CC BY 2.0 Generic

Chimpanzees live in groups called communities. Chimpanzee communities can contain 20 to more than 150 chimpanzees! There are smaller groups within a community of chimpanzees. These smaller groups usually have 6-7 members that travel and stay together for a while. Some chimps in small groups leave the group and join another one. Therefore the members of a small group always change.

# Communication

Photo by Indo_girl2010 (flickr.com/jen_lipp), as licensed under CC BY 2.0 Generic

Chimpanzees communicate with each other through sounds, hand gestures and facial expressions. Chimpanzees have cries that can warn others of danger from 2 miles away! They also bark loudly to call others to a feast and drum on trees. Chimpanzees have friendly, angry, worried, frightened and other facial expressions. They will also hold their two hands out to beg for food. Friend chimpanzees often hold hands, hug each other, and even kiss.

# Grooming

Photo by Brian Harries (flickr.com/129936023@N02), as licensed under CC BY 2.0 Generic

Chimpanzees clean each other's hair a lot. This is known as grooming. Chimpanzees scratch one another's hair to remove dirt, dead skin, and parasites. They also clean cuts and scratches if there are any. Grooming is very important for chimps and it takes up most of their resting time. Grooming helps the chimpanzee relationships grow stronger. Chimpanzees sometimes take turns grooming each other, and on other times they form a long line of chimps grooming each other!

# Breeding

Chimpanzees will mate any time of the year. Female chimpanzees mate with several males. Male chimpanzees treat all young in their community as their own because there is no way to know for sure which is theirs. Chimpanzees usually give birth to only one baby at a time. Female chimpanzees don't mate again until their child is grown. This usually takes five years.

# Baby Chimpanzees

Photo by pelican (flickr.com/pelican), as licensed under CC BY-SA 2.0 Generic

Female chimpanzees give birth after 8.5 to 9 months. Newborn baby chimpanzees are born helpless and they cling on to their mother's belly for 30 days. After about six months, baby chimpanzees will start riding on their mother's back. Baby chimpanzees start to walk and sit independently when they reach two years old, but they still depend on their mother until they reach about 5 years old.

# Life of a Chimpanzee

When a chimpanzee reaches six years old, they will still remain close to their mother but have other interactions with other chimpanzees. Adolescent females move between small groups of chimpanzees and adolescent males spend time with adult males in hunting and boundary patrolling. Female chimpanzees can start reproducing at 13 years old, but males are not considered adults until they reach 16 years old. Wild chimpanzees usually live 35 to 40 years, but in captivity they can live up to 60 years!

# What the Chimpanzee Eats

Chimpanzees are omnivores. This means that they eat vegetables and meat. Different fruits are the chimpanzee's favorite food. They will look for fruits even if there is little fruit around. They also eat leaves, flowers, seeds and other pant material. Chimpanzees hunt monkeys, baboons, antelopes and warthogs. They also eat honey, eggs, insects, birds and even soil!

# Hunting

Photo by Eric Kilby (flickr.com/ekilby), as licensed under CC BY-SA 2.0 Generic

Male chimpanzees do most of the hunting. Chimpanzees work together when hunting. During a hunt in the trees, chimpanzees are assigned to different tasks. "Drivers" try to keep the prey running in a certain direction. "Blockers" block the prey from moving away from the path. "Chasers" are fast moving chimpanzees that try to make a catch. And lastly "ambushers" hide and wait for the prey. They will then attack the prey when it comes close enough. Chimpanzees distribute their kill between the hunting party members and sometimes even bystanders.

# Drinking

Photo by Michael Bentley (flickr.com/donhomer), as licensed under CC BY 2.0 Generic

Chimpanzees bow down and bring their mouth to the water. But sometimes they use leaves to bring water to their mouth! Chimpanzees fold leaves, dip them in water, and quickly bring it up to their mouth while it is still very wet. Using leaves for drinking is just one of the tools chimpanzees use.

# Tools

Chimpanzees are one of the few animals known to use tools. Young chimpanzees are taught by adult chimpanzees how to perfect the using of tools. Aside from using leaves for drinking, chimpanzees use small sticks to 'fish' for termites. They use rocks as an anvil to break open hard nuts. And they even use spears! Chimpanzees can sharpen the tip of a stick with their teeth and use it to kill small animals.

# Intelligence

Photo by Steve Snodgrass (flickr.com/stevensnodgrass), as licensed under CC BY 2.0 Generic

Chimpanzees are intelligent animals. Experiments showed that they have a good memory. Chimpanzees can learn the number 1 to 9 and their values. They also can solve puzzles for entertainment. Other scientists have tried to teach chimpanzees American Sign Language. And some reports say that the chimpanzees were able to learn a little of sign language!

# Predators

Photo by nachans (flickr.com/pancakeplan), as licensed under CC BY 2.0 Generic

Chimpanzees don't have many predators because they are strong and usually stay in groups in rainforests. However, leopards are known to kill and eat some chimpanzees. And the chimpanzees that live in the savannas are also sometimes killed by lions. Other animals that can kill chimpanzees are crocodiles and giant snakes that can grow up to 20 feet long. Chimpanzees use large sticks or

branches to throw at their
enemies like leopards or
humans!

# Endangered

Photo by Josh Grenier (flickr.com/jdg32373), as licensed under CC BY 2.0 Generic

There aren't very many chimpanzees left in the wild anymore, and chimpanzee numbers are steadily decreasing. This is because humans are chopping down the trees in the rainforests where chimpanzees live. Some people also kill and eat chimpanzees illegally. Another reason why chimpanzees are endangered is diseases. Chimpanzees can catch many of the same diseases as humans.

# Common Chimpanzee

There are two species of chimpanzee, common chimpanzee and a bonobo. Although the word 'chimpanzee' can be used to refer to the two species, it is usually understood to be referring to the common chimpanzee only.

# Bonobo

Bonobos can only be found in Congo. They are distinguished by their relatively long legs, pink lips, and dark face. Bonobos are very similar to common chimpanzees. There are only a few differences between the two including what they look like, behavior, and where they live.

# Get the next book in this series!

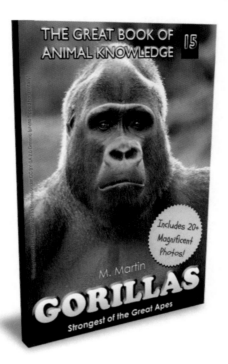

## GORILLAS: Strongest of the Great Apes

Log on to Facebook.com/GazelleCB for more info

Tip: Use the key-phrase "The Great Book of Animal Knowledge" when searching for books in this series.

For more information about our books, discounts and updates, please Like us on Facebook!

Facebook.com/GazelleCB

Made in the USA
Lexington, KY
16 December 2016